21 Whispers

Pages from Poet's Diary

Dr. Jaya Sweta Srivastava

Dedication

I am overjoyed to dedicate this poetry collection to my wonderful husband, Anupam Srivastava. Your unwavering support has transformed my life and encouraged me to reach new heights in my writing and personal growth. You have been my rock and greatest inspiration in quiet moments and joyful celebrations. Your belief in me ignites my passion and motivates me to pursue my dreams wholeheartedly.

To my cherished children, Kashish and Leo, you are the centre of my universe. Kashish taught me my first lessons in motherhood, and Leo's arrival was a precious gift to us all. You both have shown me what it means to love unconditionally, filling our home with laughter and joy. Your unique perspectives and boundless curiosity inspire me daily, and I am honoured to be your mother.

I am deeply grateful to my father, Anil Kumar Vidyarithy, for instilling the invaluable habit of journaling in me. This practice has nurtured my personal and artistic growth. Your belief in my potential since childhood has encouraged me to share my voice with the world.

To my remarkable mother, Dr. Bandana Vidyarithy, your faith in me has been a constant source of inspiration. You have always urged me to chase my dreams, no matter how distant they seem. Your love for storytelling ignited my writing journey, and I am forever grateful for that.

I dearly remember my late brother, Rahul Bhaiya, whose spirit comforts me during tough times. I also fondly recall my grandparents: Dadaji—Late Sri Vibhuti Prasad and Dadi Ma—Late Smt. Susheela Prasad, Nanaji—Late Sri Prem Shankar Prasad, and Nani—Late Smt. Prameela Prasad. I believe the wonderful story times during summer vacations instilled this skill in me. My late father-in-law, Sri Hariom Prakash Srivastava, and my mother-in-law, Srimati Sashi Srivastava, inspired me with their love and values. Though they left us too soon, their blessings will always protect us.

My sister, Mrs. Rashmi Saxena, deserves special mention for teaching me courage and resilience, and my brother-in-law, Dr. Ashish Saxena, whose encouragement has guided me through challenges. To my younger brother, Mayank, your honest insights and unwavering support have been crucial to my growth as a writer, and my Sister inlaw Sameeksha, for your unending love and appreciation.

I also dedicate this book to our family's powerhouse: my lovely nieces and nephews, Shashwat, Rishika, Little Princess Tinker, the bundle of joy, Vaibhav, Samarth, Anamika, and Shaurya, whose love generates the energy for my work.

This dedication also extends to my cousin, Mr. Prakhar Raj, who holds a special place in my heart. You have been a beacon of joy and companionship, especially after losing Rahul Bhaiya. Your kindness and support mean the world to me.

I deeply thank my teachers, mentors, and colleagues for shaping my journey with their invaluable lessons. Most importantly, to my readers: Your engagement with my poetry motivates me to explore deeper feelings and experiences, pushing me onward in my creative journey.

Finally, I dedicate this book to the Almighty, through whom I can share my thoughts and emotions with the world. Thank you all for being a part of my journey.

Preface

All 21 poems in this collection are unique and infused with profound meanings from my life experiences and lessons. They invite you on an emotional journey through relationships and self-discovery, encouraging you to laugh, cry, and feel those exhilarating goosebumps. I am excited for you to read them and gain a fresh perspective on life.

Each poem tells its own story, and I assure you you will find your journey reflected in them. You will witness the full spectrum of life and confront a reality that resonates within my words. My language is straightforward and accessible, ensuring a connection with everyone.

As a child, I often stood before a mirror, pouring out my heart and capturing my innermost thoughts in a diary my father gave me. This practice revealed to me that my words held significant depth and insight.

The loss of my older brother, with whom I shared a deep bond, and my beloved grandmother, whom I called Dadi Ma, was a pivotal moment in my life. The shock of these losses inspired me to gaze at the stars—a theme that permeates my poetry.

I also cherish my strong relationships with my husband's friends and their wives, which inspired a chapter titled "Framily." While my poetry often focuses on women's empowerment, I firmly believe that the essence of being a woman is incomplete without the presence of men; together, they complement one another beautifully. Life is not a competition; it's about the invaluable lessons both genders can impart to each other.

My poetry conveys strong messages about marriage and the principles I learned through my experiences after my husband entered my life. Our union, arranged by our parents and rooted in tradition, reminds me that the younger generation must rediscover the institution of marriage. My work highlights the powerful bond that exists between husband and wife.

My daughter, Kashish, is a constant source of inspiration for my poems on motherhood. She is my first wish and my last desire; ultimately, she will determine whether I have succeeded or failed as a parent.

You will also witness my transformation in these poems —from being afraid of animals to embracing the joy of being a pet parent, thanks to Leo, my cherished companion.

My spiritual connections and thoughts on life, death, and karma will offer you different perspectives that may be familiar but are presented with a fresh touch. Empowering poems on womanhood will surely inspire you to dream and create a glorious future.

I am confident you will enjoy my poetry and connect with the deep emotions behind each piece. Thank you for welcoming my book into your library.

Acknowledgements

I want to take this opportunity to acknowledge and express my heartfelt gratitude for the incredible experience I had while writing my 21 poems. Each represents a creative endeavour and a deeply personal journey that has enriched my life in countless ways.

First and foremost, I extend my sincere thanks to Book Leaf Publication. Your support and encouragement allowed me to pour my emotions onto the page and share my poetic voice with the world. The 21-day poetry challenge was not just an assignment but a transformative process that allowed me to explore the depths of my thoughts and feelings, ultimately creating meaningful, lasting art.

I am immensely grateful to my husband, Mr. Anupam Srivastava. Your unwavering love and belief in my abilities have been my guiding light. Your encouragement pushed me to pursue my passion and remain steadfast despite self-doubt. This journey would not have been the same without your support.

To my beloved parents and siblings, thank you for your unwavering faith in my artistic journey. Your constant encouragement has shaped my confidence and motivated me to chase my dreams relentlessly. I honour my ancestors and strive to carry on their legacy while making you all proud with every word I pen.

I would also like to take a moment to remember my late father-in-law, Sri Hariom Prakash Srivastava, and my late mother-in-law, Smt. Shashi Srivastava. When I joined your family, I felt a warm embrace of love and support. Your belief in me is a cherished memory that inspires my creativity and fuels my passion. My connection with Anupam and your everlasting presence in my life are gifts I hold close to my heart.

Lastly, a heartfelt thank you to my readers. Your willingness to engage with my work and immerse yourself in my poetry means more than words can express. I hope my poems resonate with you, evoke emotions, and provide insights that enrich your lives. Your support is the backbone of my artistic journey, and I am genuinely grateful to share this experience with you.

With each poem, I aim to express my deepest thoughts and emotions and create a legacy that inspires future generations—especially my daughter, Kashish. Your encouragement helps me honour our family name and keep our story alive. Thank you all for being such an integral part of my journey!

1. Life Lesson's... My way to learn

Life is a beautiful lesson, rich in expression,
It was an incredible journey, filled with every kind of
session.

Everything you witness is a broadcast of truth,
At the right moment, it will reveal its proof.

Everyone has a story, unique and profound,
Some are uplifting, others may astound.

For some, life is awe-inspiring and bright,
For others, it's challenges that ignite the fight.

For some, it's about teaching and the joy of learning,
For others, it's daily earnings, a fire that's burning.

For some, it's an aura of love, shining clear,
For others, it's emotions bought and sold year by year.

Some are born with golden spoons, wealth in their hand,
While others juggle loans, making the best of their
stand.

Some see abundance and dreams that gleam,
For others, it's fear and struggle that interrupt the
dream.

Compromises and sacrifices are part of the game,
But choices shape the journey; they hold the same
claim.

For some, life is high tides followed by lows,
While others experience life as a thrilling roller coaster
flows.

Family and friends bring joy, warmth, and cheer,
For some, loneliness can feel all too near.

Some celebrate daily, with joy in their stride;
Others face disheartenment; still, they abide.

There's no balance or equality; that's the karmic way,
But embrace the smiles, even on a woeful day.

Acknowledge that tears can accompany delight,
For life is a canvas, vibrant and bright.

Stick to what you choose, whether it's fuss or buzz,
All emotions await; it's up to us.

Don't mask the truth with emotions you paint,
Instead, express your essence—let your spirit not faint.

Life is a rainbow with colours that blend,
Craft a meaningful canvas; let the journey transcend.

2. Dare to dream- spiritual conversation of Life & Death....

Life once asked under the cosmic sky,
"Dear Death, can you dare to dream and reach high?"

With a gentle smile, Death replied with grace,
"Nothing dares more than my eternal embrace."

"Remember, dear Life, while you pursue the bright light,
In your dreams, I linger, guiding you through the night.

You chase fleeting shadows, illusions that sway,
Yet I am the truth that shall never decay."

Life pondered softly, "But where do you stay?
I am felt in laughter, in the warmth of the day.

I am seen and heard; in vibrant hues, I glow.
Oh, Death, my dear friend, where do you go?"

Death spoke with wisdom as the stars twinkled bright,
"When I emerge from the shadows, you shall fade from
sight.

Once my presence is known, your whispers will cease,
And in the silence of eternity, you shall find peace."

"But in my heart, there's beauty that people hold dear;
In their hopes and wishes, it is I they revere."

With tear-filled eyes, Death spoke with care,
"Those who truly know, pray for my tender snare."

Life's heart ached gently, embracing the truth;
Death is not a rival but a bridge in her youth.

They are threads in the fabric of the cosmic design,
Intertwined destinies, a divine dance.

"We were born together, a sacred decree,"
Death whispered, "Your first breath set me free.

Each heartbeat a journey, each moment a gift,
Towards my warm embrace, your spirit shall drift."

In the cycle of living and the grace of release,

A beautiful loop is created where souls find their peace.

Life wrapped her arms around Death in a tender
embrace,
Feeling love in the earth and enlightenment's grace.

Together, they ventured in harmony and light,
Two eternal forces in the depths of the night.

Within this grand journey, they both play their part,
Life and Death, a dance of the spirit and heart.

3. Reaching Perfection through the path of imperfect action.

My loving child, I've seen your flaws,
In every step you take, laughter and pause.

Even when you were not in the world's view,
We shared unsung stories, which were so precious and
true.

When you lacked the warm embrace of an arm,
My womb held you close, cradled your charm.

In the playground's absence, your spirit took flight,
I felt your little kicks throughout the night.

When your heartbeat softly, tethered to mine,
I cherished each whisper, a love so divine.

Before you crawled, I kept you near,

Wrapped in my shawl, the world felt so clear.

But you learned to walk, to run with delight,
Each step was a celebration, a dance in the light.

When your words were simple to those who would hear,
I cherished each sound, a melody dear.

As you learned to speak, to share, and to play,
I beamed with pride, watching you forge your own way.

When you splashed in colours, feeling quite free,
I marvelled at the artwork your giggles would see.

To you, they may seem like chaos and mess,
But to me, they are treasures—pure love, I confess.

I adored your naughtiness, rejoiced in your cheer,
You filled my world with colours so dear.

I watched you grow, saw you start to crawl,
Felt your happiness in each rise and fall.

Whether skating or diving beneath the cool blue,
I saw how you learned and how each challenge grew.

As the first left-handed child in our fold,

Your journey was tough, but your spirit was bold.

With every stroke, you crafted your art,
Eventually, writing with strength from the heart.

Pretending a stethoscope in your small hand,
Declaring you're a doctor, as bright as you stand.

You are our lifeline, our ray of pure hope,
In the darkness, you'll shine, helping us cope.

There are countless stories still waiting to be told,
But for now, my child, know you're precious as gold.

Through every flaw and each step that you take,
Perfection awaits as you learn from each mistake.

4. Sweet 16 vs. Crazy '40s

Oh, the sweet age of sixteen, where life feels like a
dream,
You're a bright-eyed caterpillar bursting at the seams!

While I'm in my forties, feeling slightly more bee-like,
Gathering up wisdom, but honey, do I think the spike!

You dive headfirst into friendship; oh, what a delight,
Exploring the maze of life, dancing into the night.

I'm over here sifting through memories like old clothes,
Trusting only a few circles slowly shrinks and grows.

You run, and you tumble, learning with each fall,
While I'm over here thinking, "Should I risk it at all?"

You're in springtime bliss, with flowers all around,
While autumn nips at my heels, with leaves on the
ground.

You're buying up dreams like candy from a store,
But my dreams are like socks—missing and lost, and
maybe more!

You've got gadgets and gizmos, all shiny and new,
I'm still working on my flip phone, which has issues, too!

Oh, the drama of puberty—your moods swing like a
door,
While I'm riding the waves of menopause, praying for
calm at the shore.

You're colouring those tresses with hues bold and
bright,
While I'm embracing the grey—what a sight, what a
sight!

You're out making memories, with laughter and cheers,
While at home, I'm munching snacks, battling my fears.

I think back to my youth, my thrill-seeking ways,
I wonder if this trusty couch is where I'll spend my days.

This generation gap stretches out like a long scarf,
With each of us laughing, trying not to start a war of the
heart.

Your mom was once my age, dancing to the same beat,
Oh, sweet child, someday you'll know what this means,
bittersweet!

But here's the truth that tugs on my soul,
Your happiness and safety are what make me whole.

Let's stand side by side, reflecting in the glass,
Embracing our quirks and each crazy moment that will
pass.

For you're sweet sixteen, full of sass and cheer,
And I'm crazy at forty-two—cheers to laughter and a
little fear!

So, let's celebrate this journey with a wink and a grin,
In the awkward dance of life, let the laughter begin!

5. LEO & the golden glow-Emotions in Fur.

In our lives, Leo arrived, a bundle of joy,
A gift for my daughter, far more than just a toy.

With sparkling eyes and a beaming face,
He rushed through life, eager to win the race.

His tail wagged wildly after each daring feat,
Melting our hearts, no matter our mood's heat.

With a humble nature, he transformed our days,
Caring and loyal, he truly deserves praise.

He asks for so little—a walk, some food, and play;
In return, a hug chases our troubles away.

When he's unwell, he knows just what to say;
His joy at mealtime reflects love's gentle ballet.

He connects with all, drawing attention near;

With his pleading puppy face, how could we not cheer?

On sandy beaches, he runs, splashing in glee,
Teaching us life's lessons—oh, how sweet it can be.

I'm not sure when I shifted from owner to friend;
I can't picture a future where our paths don't blend.

He's my companion, bringing solace and peace;
In his warm embrace, all my worries cease.

My golden retriever, the sweetest of souls,
He makes our family whole as together we stroll.

From tiny beginnings, I used to fear;
Now our strong bond is built on love sincere.

When I felt unwell, sorrow filled his eyes;
In shared moments of heart, our connection lies.

I remember the days when I'd say, "Not for me,"
Now, Leo has shown me how to love fearlessly.

So here's to you, Leo, let's play and rejoice;
In the dance of our lives, you'll always be my choice.

A beautiful bond, forever we'll share;
In the footsteps of love, we breathe the same air.

6. Sheroes -The Lady heroes

Have you ever heard of a lady hero, a "shero"?
She is everywhere, deserving recognition, never a zero.

Often overlooked, but she's powerful and strong,
When given the chance, she proves critics wrong.

With unwavering pride and determination, she soars,
Her worth is immeasurable; she opens doors.

No longer hiding in shadows, she steps into the light,
The tough times are behind her; now, she shines bright.

In tales of old and real life today,
She stands tall and bold, paving her way.

Faced with challenges, she breaks down the walls,
"This is not the end," she proudly calls.

Though she has stumbled, she continuously stands,
Finding joy in the sunshine, embracing life's plans.

In every realm, you will find her grace,
A fierce leader, a nurturer in every place.

Do not underestimate the strength she brings;
Stand beside her—together, you can take on anything.

Whether at home or in the workplace space,
She's a relentless warrior, claiming her place.

Like an ant, she perseveres, never backs down,
You can't hold her back; she'll wear her crown.

Breaking free from the ordinary, she'll take to the skies,
Singing songs that inspire, letting her spirit rise.

This isn't about trophies or glory on display;
She seeks your support in a meaningful way.

So when you see her, give her a cheer,
Let's celebrate that incredible shero, so near!

She is a shero, radiating confidence and light,
Rarely acknowledged, but always ready to fight.

Once held back, now she's ready to amaze,
Watch her rise and shine, deserving all praise.

7. Gazing eyes -oh No! Madam again.

When I look back through the pages of my past,
I can't forget those faces; their memories hold fast.

As a professor at university , it was quite the journey,
An adventure filled with laughter, growth, and a hint of
worry.

Those days were a blast, teaching future engineers,
Nurturing their minds while confronting their fears.

I was tough as nails, my standards set high,
Many would tremble, and some would even sigh.

"We're in college, madam, not in basic school!"
With playful despair, they'd declare, "You're such a rule!"

Yet beneath their grumbles, I could see the spark,
A thirst for knowledge igniting in the dark.

Oh, the moments of tension when secrets were kept,
Students stealing glances, a whirlwind adept.

In hushed whispers, they'd plan their sly chance,
Caught in the thrill of their youthful dance.

"Two more minutes, please, we're not quite prepared!"
I chuckled; oh yes, I knew they were scared.

In their hearts, a hope, on test day, they'd bet,
"Oh no, it's her again!" they'd jest with regret.

Now, on social media, they reach out with glee,
Sharing their stories—what a joy it brings me!

Apologizing for antics, some foolish, some fun,
Yet through all the chaos, we forged a bond.

I wish them the best in all their endeavour,
With dreams in their hearts, may they soar forever.

It fills me with joy to remember our lively crew,
For in every goodbye, a part of me stays with you.

8. Myth of perfect mom: Celebrating imperfection.

why do we expect perfection from our mother?
Although she shines in her beautiful reflection.

Every lesson learned in her childhood
Is woven into motherhood with love and affection.

Her heart holds countless lessons,
Each one is embraced with tides of emotions.

In every moment, she pours out her love,
Even when she feels she hasn't reached the perfect mark.

Though a child may not always get realised,
Mom remains aware she might not get criticised

To be her best self, she embraces struggles,
Carrying dreams and hopes nestled in her heart anew.

Life is a journey they embark on together,

Navigating the waters of life's grand adventure.

Day by day, they explore their individuality,
Creating a unique story as they both grow.

Together, they cherish roles beautifully intertwined,
Thriving in a bond that is sacred and kind.

Embracing the truth that perfection isn't required,
She moves with grace, her spirit inspired.

Every mom draws from vast experiences,
Adapting and evolving, each moment a blast.

Imparting wisdom to the next generation,
Understanding that life is more than an examination.

No mom can ever be perfect; it's true,
A resonant fact that empowers her too.

In her little imperfections lies her true strength,
And through her boundless love, she triumphs at length.

9. A day with Bunny: Crazy Days, Sweet Nights with a Hop, a Skip, a Smile

In a tale of guests and hosts, unwanted fears arise,
A tiny creature, a furry ghost, surprised me with its eyes.

Now it seems a funny tale, but then my heart raced wild,
A tightened jaw and a quickened pulse—I was a
frightened child.

One sunny day, my daughter returned, a mischievous
delight,
Holding a big packet, she whispered, "Mom, it's quite a
sight."

"Open the door, come inside," she urged with glee,
"A bunny's here as an assignment; don't be scared of
me!"

"What have you in your hands?" I gasped, astonished

and perplexed,
"A bunny!" she exclaimed, while my mind became vexed.

"How could the school send a pet without my consent?"
Though love for animals was the lesson, my heart was
far from content.

In anger, I opened the door, "Keep it on the balcony," I
said,
Then, I rushed to call my husband, fears racing in my
head.

As I called, the tears flowed, my voice trembled with
fright,
He promised he'd be home soon, trying to make sense of
my plight.

Phobias dominate my heart, of tiny creatures near,
And how my daughter dared to act filled me with panic
and fear.

A knock then broke the silence—it was my daughter, so
sad,
Her guilty tears melted my heart, a feeling both happy
and bad.

She'd known I'd be afraid, yet love for pets would sway,

When I came out to help, the bunny needed care that
day.

With a bowl of water and a carrot, I offered a treat,
Through the window, I watched him munch, such a
charming sight, so sweet.

On one side stood my daughter, the bunny in delight,
On the other, I stood frozen in a humorous plight.

When my husband arrived, tension hung in the air,
His anger flared for my daughter, filled with loving care.

"Return him the next day," my daughter promised him
tight,
So that night, we kept the guest in our home, a
whimsical sight.

The bunny danced and frolicked under the moonlight's
soft glow,
With muddy paws, he claimed the night; his joy began to
grow.

Sleep eluded us that night, as laughter mixed with fright,
My husband and daughter cleaned till the dawn's early
light.

The bunny, scared yet loved, found warmth in their
embrace,
Cocooned in cuddles and dreams in my daughter's gentle
space.

The next day came to say goodbye, to send him back to
school,
No pets in our house would be the new golden rule.

The mess on the terrace—a sight that made me sigh,
My maid's fury was palpable when I asked her to
comply.

All day, I pondered, feeling sorrowful and sad—
Though I saw him as unwanted, he brought joy that was
rad.

A guest in our lives, though for me he was a plight,
For my daughter's first pet, her happiness felt so right.

Those shiny eyes during farewell left me speechless,
wondering why,
A twinge of guilt at taking joy from her made me sigh.

For in that tiny creature, a bond had grown somehow,
I learned that love can blossom, even in fear's shadowed
vow.

10. Its me again! Falling Stars, Rising Dreams

Standing before the mirror's gaze,
I recognized a face from brighter days.

A closer look revealed the pain,
Wounds hidden deep, like teardrops of rain.

She wrestles with the weight of choice;
This isn't an end—just a pause in her voice.

With fierce resolve, she finds her power,
Proclaiming boldly, "It's me, in this hour!"

It's a mystery why doubt takes hold,
When she balances life, steadfast and bold.

With determination, she conquers the steep,
Turning the impossible into hopes she can keep.

If her family supports her as she dares to soar,

Her light will shine bright and be recognized evermore.

But when the storms crash and the shadows grow,
She'll choose warmth at home, letting the fame go.

At times, she yearns for the love she deserves,
An embrace of attention that always preserves.

Her heart craves acknowledgement, bold and profound,
When doubt whispers, she stands her ground.

Whether to work or nurture her home,
She'll make her choice and no longer roam.

Not a puppet in strings, but the maker of fate,
She'll cherish her dreams and never hesitate.

Her love for others, a treasure untold;
Her eyes share stories that remain uncontrolled.

Though fears may haunt her late in the night,
She courageously shouts, "It's me, shining bright!"

11. Lost Souls in the Night Sky:Glimmers of those we miss.

When I was young and lost in sorrow's grasp,
I turned to my mother, seeking answers to the clasp.

"Where have they gone?" I whispered in the night,
She pointed to the stars, twinkling so bright.

"All those shining gems are your ancestors near,
Embrace their glow, for they'll always be here."

In my heart, I wove a story, a comforting thread,
Believing those stars were my loved ones, now dead.

Whenever I was sad, I'd look up and sigh,
Talking to the cosmos, letting my worries fly.

They never judged me; they healed scars,
In the depths of darkness, I found solace in stars.

I named them all gently, discovered their light,
Their familiar faces emerging through the night.

In moments of trouble, I sought their wise grace,
Finding peace in their brilliance, my sacred space.

Sometimes love is a language that words cannot speak,
A bond that transcends, though we may feel weak.

Surrounded by many, yet feeling so alone,
Longing for companionship, craving a home.

In a crowd of voices, I search for that friend,
Who understands my silence, who'll be there 'til the end.

When the world feels heavy, and I need to confide,
I gaze at the stars, where my heart can abide.

"Hello there," I send them, in whispers and sighs,
Their shimmering glow answers all my "whys."

In the warmth of their light, I find comfort anew,
For in every bright star, I feel love shining through.

12. "Framily" beyond friendship, part of family

In a world so big, with paths that twist and bend,
There are a few dear souls who feel like family, my
friend.

They're more than friends; they're my heart's delight,
With laughter and love, they make everything right.

Our bond is like magic, a treasure divine,
Every moment together is a reason to shine.

They wrap me in kindness, with hearts open wide,
There is no judgment in sight; love is our guide.

Through joy and sadness, we share every tear,
In their company, I find nothing to fear.

What a beautiful dance, this friendship is so true,
Distance fades away when I'm close to you.

As life moves us forward and our families grow,
The ties that we cherish continue to flow.

With a wink and a smile, we lift each other high,
In this circle of love, we'll always stand by.

It's a give-and-take journey, but the family knows best,
With warmth in our hearts, we stand every test.

No matter who calls first, it's the joy that we find,
In laughter and chatter, our spirits entwined.

Dial my number at three in the morning's sweet light,
I'll be there in a heartbeat, and I hope you support me in
the night.

With no second-guessing, just love all around,
In the term "family," our magic is found.

From the depths of our hearts, we hold each other dear,
No distance can sever this bond; that's so clear.

For many decades we've built this wonderful tale,
And it will echo forever, a love that won't fail.

13. "Traditional Ties with bond of love"A Journey of Love with 2 Decade of togetherness.

Nearly two decades have flown like a gentle breeze,
Since we embarked together, hearts entwined with ease.

An arranged union, yet a tapestry so grand,
Woven with threads of fate, guided by love's hand.

Your first picture took my breath, stole my dreams away,
In that moment, career goals seemed to fade and sway.

We were two distinct souls, with worlds apart,
Yet the magic of opposites ignited my heart.

In your green shirt, you stood, a vision divine,
Eyes sparkling like stars, your charm made me resign

To the shyness within, as you lit up my night,
You were my serendipity, my guiding light.

Through the Times Matrimony, our paths intertwined,
Families wrote our story, yet love we soon would find.

As our nuptial knot was tied, a new chapter began,
From characters on paper to a shared life plan.

The moment our rings exchanged, my world
transformed,
In your hand, I felt a love that would keep me warm.

As we walked around the fire, our dreams took flight,
Those seven sacred steps sealed our bond that night.

Through every high and low, in a village or city,
I wear the title of your Mrs., a crown of pure beauty.

As we took our seven vows, with blessings from above,
When you placed vermilion on my head, I found true
love.

Years have passed like fleeting clouds across the sky,
Yet my heart knows the depth of love that will never die.

What began as an arrangement has grown into
something rare,
A remarkable connection, a love beyond compare.

Together, we've crafted a life rich and true,
It was a beautiful journey filled with laughter and trust
anew.

In the tapestry of existence, hand in hand we weave,
An endless story of love, together we believe.

14. Dreams Take Flight: Turning Pages at Eighteen

As you turn eighteen, my precious girl,
Embrace the world that awaits to unfurl,

Let your dreams blossom, let your spirit rise,
With each step you take, trust the heart that lies.

Hold close the laughter from days long ago,
Those carefree moments, a warm, gentle glow.

Cherished memories, treasures untold,
Form the foundation, more precious than gold.

You are brave and bright, a beacon of light,
Chase your dreams passionately, with all of your might.

With every adventure, spread your wings wide,
The power is yours; let your courage be your guide.

When challenges come, stand tall and be strong,

My unwavering love will always help you along.

Let your spirit shine as you reach for the skies,
In all of your journeys, know you are never alone in your
rise.

So go on, dear daughter, and reach for the stars,
The world is your canvas; embrace who you are.

No dream is too distant, no hope out of sight,
Trust the magic within you—your future is bright.

With our shared memories lighting your way,
You'll navigate life with courage each day.

Chase your dreams fiercely; let your heart lead the
dance,
I'll always be here, cheering on your chance.

15. joy of spreading smile

I walked along a bustling street one day,
And saw a mother in dismay,

Holding her child, who longed for a treat,
Their eyes spoke of hunger on that crowded street.

She looked so helpless, perhaps cashless too,
While I was in my car, thoughts racing through,

Rushing to the office, skipping my lunch,
Nibbling a sandwich in a hurried crunch.

But that sight tugged at my heart,
A reminder of struggle, a painful part.

I called to the lady with a heart full of cheer,
To give her my sandwich was a gesture of sincerity.

The smiles they exchanged filled the air with light,
A moment of joy in a world full of plight.

In the mother's eyes, a sigh of relief,
A slice of compassion, a break from her grief.

Though the day was hectic, I found pure bliss,
In that simple act, I discovered a gift.

I wish to share, as this lesson I glean,
Spread joy to the world. Let kindness be seen.

Life's a treasure meant to be shared,
To lift the fallen, to show that we care.

We can't change their past or their fate,
But in this moment, we can elevate.

Small acts of kindness may seem so slight,
Yet they can ignite someone's spirit, ignite their light.

These gestures of goodwill enrich us all,
Every smile we create is a powerful call.

So let's spread joy with each step we take,
Brighten the world, for kindness's sake.

In every small gesture and connection we find,
Together we rise, with love intertwined.

16. Race to Reach on the top

In a world where all are racing to the crest,
As if happiness is just a trinket, a fleeting guest.

So consumed by gold, they neglect to see
Life drifts away like grains of sand by the sea,

With each breath, a reminder that time is a thief,
And the final curtain falls, often beyond belief.

What is this mountain that beckons so boldly?
Once reached, do they find terror instead of glory?

Will the insatiable thirst for "more" ever abate,
Or will future souls follow this relentless fate?

At the summit, I see countless pallid faces;
Youth and true joy are lost in this ceaseless race.

Though winning can shine, the top's light is dim;
Yet we've been taught that the peak is the hymn.

How unfairly we label each stumble a sin,
Society engraves it; this pressure we're in.

Countless lives breaking beneath this cruel weight,
Yet the cries for change too often abate.

People speak of a view that takes breath away,
But loneliness lingers as friends fall astray.

For among the pretenders, the heartache is real,
And the cost of ambition is often concealed.

Perhaps it's more noble to master many trades,
Then, to chase just one star that might quickly fade.

For if, as a master, one should misstep or fall,
What options remain when the writing's on the wall?

At the pinnacle's edge, authenticity wanes;
In the rush for the summit, we risk genuine gains.

So let us reflect as we scale these grand heights,
True allies and happiness are our greatest rights.

17. unconditional love

True love is never conditional; it is a powerful force.
It creates an exceptional connection that charts its own
course.

It's divine, like a beacon, unshaken by the night,
Yet sometimes, it can leave you feeling lost in its light.

It cannot be defined or confined in a box,
A whirlwind of feelings, like keys to a box of locks.

It offers clarity, guiding you through,
But at times, it brings heartache and makes you blue.

It fiercely protects your dreams, standing by your side,
Yet whispers of sacrifice can be hard to abide.

With every sweet gesture, it lifts you so high,
But it can also ground you, making you sigh.

It shows you the path, yet where does it lead?
Through valleys of joy and the thorns of greed.

Love is a soft whisper, then a thunderous call;
It nurtures your spirit but can also let you fall.

Seamless in beauty, yet tangled in thread,
Timeless and ageless, it shapes the life we've led.

A tapestry is woven with joy and fear;
In the end, it's true love—ever precious and dear.

True love is a force both powerful and pure,
An unwavering bond that stands strong and sure.

It shines like a beacon, guiding through the night,
Yet, in its brilliance, it may dim your own light.

Unconfined by labels, it dances in the air,
A whirlwind of emotions, igniting passion's flare.

With clarity, it leads, casting shadows aside,
Yet it can also bring heartache—a storm you cannot hide.

Fierce in its protection, it stands by your side,
But whispers of sacrifice are often hard to abide.

Each gentle gesture lifts you to the skies,
Yet, in its weight, your heart sometimes sighs.

It opens new pathways, but where do they go?
Through valleys of laughter or thorns that cut low.

Love is a soft whisper, then a powerful call,
Nurturing the spirit while allowing you to fall.

Seamless in beauty, yet tangled in thread,
Timeless and ageless, it shapes the life we've led.

A tapestry is woven with joy and fear;
In the end, it's true love—ever precious and dear.

18. God is my saviour

In the embrace of the divine, I discover my grace,
A serene presence that wraps around me, creating my
sacred space.

With every challenge that life sends my way,
I walk forward with courage, knowing He is with me,
come what may.

He empowers me with strength, making me a warrior so
bold,
Amid battles, it is His eternal truths that I behold.

Each whisper of guidance, like a soft breeze, calls to my
soul,
With His unwavering presence by my side, I feel
genuinely whole.

He lifts me high on wings of radiant light,
Guiding me through the darkest valleys, where He
shines ever bright.

Every question I carry, heavy upon my heart,
In His love, I find the answers, wisdom gracefully
imparts.

When paths are obscured, and the roads seem unkind,
He carves out a way forward, with purpose finely
aligned.

In the ever-flowing river of life, His blessings abound,
Creating an endless stream of hope, where boundless
love can be found.

With love nestled deep in my heart and faith as my
guide,
I journey through the twists of life with God steadfast by
my side.

With each step I bravely take, in His presence I dwell,
Embracing a life rich with wonder, a profound story to
tell.

In moments of doubt, when my strength may wane,
I remember His promises, that through Him, I can
remain.

He nurtures my spirit, fills my soul with light,

Encouraging me to rise, to reach new heights.

With gratitude flowing freely, I cherish each day,
Acknowledging the beauty in the smallest things that
come my way.

From the laughter of friends to the quiet of the night,
Every experience is woven with His divine light.

So, as I walk this path, guided by His hand,
I trust in His purpose, His perfect plan.

With a heart full of hope and a spirit so free,
I celebrate this journey, knowing He walks with me. .

19. Everyone has a chapter, no one reads it aloud.

In each life, a chapter awaits to unfold,
A unique journey filled with stories untold.

Yet often, these narratives linger in shadow,
Unheard and unseen, treasures postponed.

I choose to share my journey with grace,
Crafting words that reflect my heart's gentle pace.

In hopes of remembrance, I deeply aspire,
To leave a legacy, a flickering fire.

May future generations, with curiosity, seek
To understand my essence, both profound and meek.

Through the trials I faced and the triumphs I gained,
In the garden of memories, the lessons remain.

Each moment of joy, each struggle and tear

Shapes who I am; I hope they will hear.

For within my stories lies wisdom and peace,
A compass for them, a guide that won't cease.

In a world that rushes, where voices can blend,
I strive to leave echoes that will never end.

With every carefully crafted line, I share my truth,
Infusing my thoughts with timeless spirit and youth.

When my voice, rich with emotion, sings in the refrain,
I hope it resonates like a soft, gentle rain.

The warmth of my laughter, the weight of my sighs,
Will linger in hearts and light up the skies.

Through this delicate balance, I find my way,
Aspiring to touch souls, come what may.

For even in absence, may my hopes endure;
In cherished connections, our love will stay pure.

As the pages of time slowly turn and unfold,
I trust my legacy will continue to be told.

A thread in the fabric of family and kin,

Binding us together, where love can begin.

With every story shared, and every lesson imparted,
I lay down foundations where dreams can be started.

So let my words be a bridge that connects,
A pathway of understanding that deeply reflects.

In this journey of life, I wish to inspire,
To kindle a flame in hearts that won't tire.

Within each chapter, there's magic to find,
A symphony of voices, a chorus intertwined.

20. Flipping Through feelings

Yesterday was a tough day; tears flowed freely,
A storm of emotions, heavy and weary.

Today shines bright, filled with laughter and joy,
Surrounded by friends, each moment we enjoy.

Their smiles lift my heart, a gentle embrace,
In this warm atmosphere, I find my place.

In this joyful moment, I feel a fresh start,
A reminder that healing begins in the heart.

Tomorrow approaches, bringing its worries,
Yet I'm wrapped in love, soothing my flurries.

The sun has been shining, bronzing my skin,
A radiant glow that reminds me to begin.

With each passing hour, I gather my strength,

Knowing that life measures its worth in length.

Embracing both day and night, I let the peace in,
Finding solace and comfort, letting new dreams begin.

In this mix of emotions, I find my way,
Navigating the highs and the lows of the day.

Every heartbeat echoes the bonds that won't fray,
Together, we stand, come what may, come what may.

So here's to the journey, with its twists and turns,
To the lessons we learn and the passion that burns.

In the tapestry of life, I weave my thread,
With hope as my compass and love as my stead.

21. Shadows of Karma

Health is our treasure, shining bright,
Guiding us through challenges, day and night.

But money worries can weigh us down,
Turning cheerful smiles into worried frowns.

On our happiest days, sadness can creep,
When memories of loss surge and leap.

Life intricately weaves joy with threads of woe,
Reminding us that both can coexist and grow.

Reflecting on the past, we find stories to tell,
Each moment is a lesson, helping us swell.

Karma spins its web with a knowing wink,
Our choices shape our paths more than we think.

In times of struggle, we summon our might,
Discovering strength in the darkest night.

Even as shadows attempt to steal our cheer,
Hope shines gently, always drawing near.

Life throws us challenges, twists of fate,
Testing our resolve, shaping what we create.

With destiny at play, we carve our road,
Transforming troubles into wisdom bestowed.

So let's raise a toast to this journey, full of surprise,
With laughter and health, let our spirits rise.

Life's a funny show with uncertainties to learn,
In this grand play, it's a joy that we yearn for.

Embrace the trials, for they're part of the game,
Each hurdle is a lesson, and each struggle is the same.

With destiny's power, we'll conquer, we'll thrive,
In the story of life, we'll truly come alive.